My Life in the
PLYMOUTH COLONY

By Max Caswell

Gareth Stevens
PUBLISHING

Please visit our website, www.garethstevens.com. For a free color catalog of all our high-quality books, call toll free 1-800-542-2595 or fax 1-877-542-2596.

Library of Congress Cataloging-in-Publication Data

Names: Caswell, Max, author.
Title: My life in the Plymouth Colony / Max Caswell.
Description: New York : Gareth Stevens Publishing, [2018] | Series: My place in history | Includes index.
Identifiers: LCCN 2017011379| ISBN 9781538203057 (pbk. book) | ISBN 9781538203064 (6 pack) | ISBN 9781538203071 (library bound book)
Subjects: LCSH: Massachusetts–History–New Plymouth, 1620-1691–Juvenile literature. | Pilgrims (New Plymouth Colony)–Juvenile literature. | Massachusetts–Social life and customs–To 1775–Juvenile literature.
Classification: LCC F68 .C295 2018 | DDC 974.4/02–dc23
LC record available at https://lccn.loc.gov/2017011379

Published in 2018 by
Gareth Stevens Publishing
111 East 14th Street, Suite 349
New York, NY 10003

Copyright © 2018 Gareth Stevens Publishing

Designer: Bethany Perl
Editor: Joan Stoltman

Photo credits: Cover, p. 1 Jennie A. Brownscombe/Wikipedia.org; cover, p. 1 (background) Natalia Sheinkin/Shutterstock.com; cover, pp. 1–24 (torn strip) barbaliss/Shutterstock.com; cover, pp. 1–24 (photo frame) Davor Ratkovic/Shutterstock.com; cover, pp. 1–24 (white paper) HABRDA/Shutterstock.com; cover, pp. 1–24 (parchment) M. Unal Ozmen/Shutterstock.com; cover, pp. 1–24 (textured edge) saki80/Shutterstock.com; pp. 1–24 (paper background) Kostenko Maxim/Shutterstock.com; p. 5 churupka/Shutterstock.com; pp. 7 (colonial kitchen), 13 (William Bradford) Bettmann/Getty Images.com; p. 7 (leading strings) Gesina ter Borch/courtesy of Rjiksmuseum; p. 9 (hornbook) Tuer/Wikipedia.org; p. 9 (Bible) Oliver Le Queinec/Shutterstock.com; p. 11 (Indian corn) Alena Haurylik/Shutterstock.com; p. 11 (main) Vaclav Volrab/Shutterstock.com; p. 13 (*Mayflower*) Barney Burstein/Corbis Historical/Getty Images; p. 15 (Sabbath) Fotosearch/Archive Photos/Getty Images; p. 15 (naughts and crosses) © iStockphoto.com/KaeArt; p. 17 (dinner prayer) Kean Collection/Archive Photos/Getty Images; p. 17 (venison) hlphoto/Shutterstock.com; p. 19 (pickled vegetables) Lestertair/Shutterstock.com; p. 19 ml1413/Shutterstock.com; p. 21 American School/Getty Images.

Printed in the United States of America

CPSIA compliance information: Batch #CS17GS: For further information contact Gareth Stevens, New York, New York at 1-800-542-2595.

CONTENTS

Words in the glossary appear in **bold** type the first time they are used in the text.

A NEW YEAR

January 1, 1633

    Every night this winter, I've worked on making my own pen, ink, and paper. I want to record life in our colony as I see it, though I'll likely never have time to write more than once a month. There's less work outside in winter, but I still have plenty of work to do inside!

    Once it's even the smallest bit warm, I'll have outdoor tasks, too. I'll have to gather nuts and berries, help with planting seeds, help with the **harvest**, and more!

Notes from History

Children in Plymouth Colony worked alongside adults starting at age 5. In order for the colony to survive, especially in its early years, everyone had to work very hard.

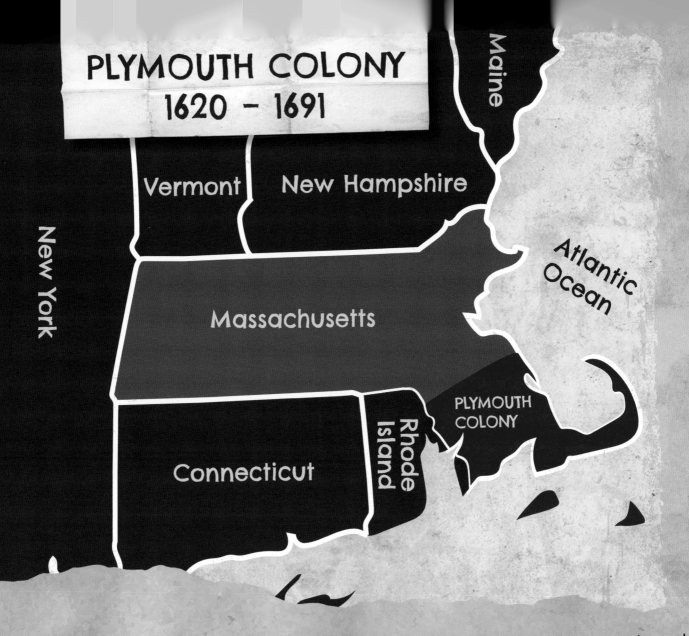

PLYMOUTH COLONY
1620 – 1691

Maine

Vermont

New Hampshire

New York

Atlantic Ocean

Massachusetts

Connecticut

Rhode Island

PLYMOUTH COLONY

Plymouth Colony began in 1620 when the *Mayflower* arrived on the east coast of what is now the state of Massachusetts. It was one of the earliest English colonies in North America.

Anne's FIRST WORD

February 6, 1633

Mother wrote me that my baby sister, Anne, spoke her first word last week. It was my name! I wish I could have been there, but I've lived with our neighbors, the Howlands, since I turned 8 this past November.

When I still lived at home, caring for Anne was how I spent my days and nights. I even held her leading strings while she learned to walk! I miss my family, but know I need to be here to learn sewing, cooking, and other skills.

Notes from History

The colonists believed parents loved and babied their children too much. They were sent away at age 8 to grow strong so they could survive the hard work in Plymouth.

LEADING STRINGS

Leading strings were often used in the 1600s to pull a baby up when they were close to falling while they learned to walk.

SCHOOLING

March 10, 1633

Mrs. Lizzie, the Howland **matriarch**, teaches me when she has free time, which isn't often. But I've learned enough that I don't need the hornbook anymore. I'm reading from the Bible now!

This spring, she'll be having her fifth child, so I need to learn as much as I can now. I practice by firelight every night after everyone's gone to sleep. If I used a candle, I'd be found out—though I don't think I'd get in much trouble for staying up to read the Bible!

Notes from History

Plymouth's first school didn't open until the 1670s. Before then, children learned to read with the only book their family owned—the Bible.

HORNBOOK

A hornbook was a wooden paddle with paper fixed to it. It was used to learn the alphabet and reading. Pages were covered with a clear, thin slice of cow's horn.

Farm LIFE

April 29, 1633

Father told me that when the colony began, no one knew how to harvest, fish, milk cows, plant crops, or anything else needed for a farm to be successful!

Our neighbors, the Wampanoag people, came and taught us how to plant Indian corn with beans and squash around it to help it grow. They also taught us to fish for herring to put in the soil under the corn seeds. Now we have Indian corn in some way with every meal!

Notes from History

Indian corn is native to North America. The Wampanoag people taught the colonists how to grow, harvest, and dry it; save seeds for the next year; and pound the rest into corn flour or corn meal.

INDIAN CORN

The Wampanoag had lived in the area for thousands of years. They also taught the colonists **crop rotation** and how to hunt.

GARDENING

May 16, 1633

Mrs. Lizzie had her child, Lydia, and so I now am in charge of tending to the vegetable garden behind the house. Because the Howlands are "old comers," **Governor** Bradford himself stopped in to see how mother and child were doing.

I'm grateful Mrs. Lizzie lived, as many women in Plymouth die during childbirth. She's a strong woman, so I'm sure she'll have many more children. For now, I will care for her parsley, carrots, turnips, and radishes.

Notes from History

Most colonists had at least 8 children, though many would die young. The real John Howland and Elizabeth "Lizzie" Tilley Howland had 10 children and now have millions of **descendants**, including three former US presidents.

THE *MAYFLOWER*

GOV. WILLIAM BRADFORD

"Old comers" were colonists who came on the *Mayflower* (1620), *Fortune* (1621), *Anne* (1623), or *Little James* (1623) ships. William Bradford, a *Mayflower* passenger with John Howland and Elizabeth Tilley, was governor of Plymouth Colony for years, helped write its first laws, and recorded its history.

The SABBATH

June 3, 1633

Our preacher spoke much of the devil's work this **Sabbath**. Several people have died of illness this summer. He told us to pray for strength to fight against the evil that was making our colony ill.

On the Sabbath, the **religious** folk of Plymouth meet twice and spend all free time in private prayer. I've also promised to spend my free time for the rest of this month in prayer and not play. No naughts and crosses, no draughts, and no lummelen for me this month.

Notes from History

In the colonists' religion, the devil was behind every bad thing, small or large, that happened. This included illness, bad weather, and more.

NAUGHTS AND CROSSES

Naughts and crosses is tic-tac-toe, draughts is checkers, and lummelen is keep away. Because they worked so much, historians aren't sure if the colony's children played games, but if they did, they would have played these games from England.

15

A FEAST

July 20, 1633

My oldest sister was married last weekend by the governor. We had quite a meal to honor the couple! Father wanted it to be special, so rather than pork or lobster, he traded for venison. The venison was cooked with gooseberries and native onions and served with toasted walnuts.

Mother made red berry pudding for a dessert course, a rare treat indeed. We dressed in our best clothes, dresses Mother made from black English cloth she had shipped here in the spring.

Notes from History

Colonists followed what was in the Bible very closely, and there were no marriage **ceremonies** in the Bible. So at Plymouth, the government, not the church, conducted these ceremonies.

VENISON

Believe it or not, lobster was actually a very common dish for the colonists. Venison, or deer meat, would have to be traded for, since the native peoples did much more hunting than the colonists.

HARVEST

August 30, 1633

Mr. John had grown enough Indian corn, oats, and wheat to sell much of it and keep our stomachs full all winter long. The Howlands will surely be able to buy plenty of sugar, salt, oil, and vinegar from Europe with this bounty! But now, the hardest work of the year must be done.

Even Mrs. Lizzie and I work in the fields now. As if we weren't busy enough drying, smoking, pickling, and **preserving** vegetables, fish, and meat for the winter, now we're collecting ears of corn!

Notes from History

Grains were often traded with nearby native groups, especially oats and wheat. In exchange, the colonists would get beaver **pelts**, which they'd trade with Europe for sugar and other things they couldn't get in Plymouth.

PICKLED VEGETABLES

One way colonists preserved food was to pickle it. Using vinegar, today you can still pickle fruits, vegetables, and even meat and fish!

BREECHING

September 16, 1633

My brother turned 7, so I returned home to see his breeching. He was very proud and happy to be rid of his "baby dress," as he called it. Many people yesterday said he looked fine in his new clothing.

He begins his training under Father now, though he'll soon become a servant in town for another family. A successful farmer must know how to plant, sow seeds, weed, tend to livestock, **butcher**, and even do woodwork. He has much to learn, just like I once did!

Notes from History

What many consider to be the first Thanksgiving occurred at Plymouth Colony sometime in the fall of 1621. The colonists and Wampanoag were celebrating a good harvest, a common event.

Men's pants were called "breeches." When a boy turned 7 and was considered old enough to dress like a man, his family hosted a "breeching" event.

GLOSSARY

butcher: to kill an animal and prepare its meat for food

ceremony: an event to honor or celebrate something

crop rotation: the practice of growing different crops on the same piece of land one season after another

descendant: a person who comes after another in a family

governor: a person who leads the government in a state, province, or colony

harvest: to bring in a crop. Also, the crop itself.

matriarch: the woman who heads a family, group, or government

pelt: the skin of a dead animal especially with its hair, wool, or fur still on it

preserve: to prevent food from rotting or breaking down by natural processes

religious: having to do with religion, a belief in and way of honoring a god or gods

Sabbath: a weekly day of rest and worship, observed on Sunday by most Christians

For more INFORMATION

Books

Allen, Nancy Kelly. *My Life as an Early Settler*. Vero Beach, FL: Rourke Educational Media, 2013.

Jones, Emma. *Recipes of the Pilgrims*. New York, NY: KidHaven Publishing, 2017.

Lynch, P. J. *The Boy Who Fell off the Mayflower, or, John Howland's Good Fortune*. Somerville, MA: Candlewick Press, 2015.

Websites

Interactive History
pbs.org/wnet/colonialhouse/history/index.html
This page includes several fun activities, including a survival quiz, an interactive map, and a dress-up game.

Virtual Field Trip
plimoth.org/learn/just-kids/virtual-field-trip
Watch two videos here, one on 17th-century English village life, and the other on Wampanoag life.

INDEX